RAPTORS!
THE NASTIEST DINOSAURS

by **Don Lessem**   Illustrated by **David Peters**

Scientific Adviser:

Dr. Philip Currie, Royal Tyrrell Museum of Palaeontology

Little, Brown and Company
Boston   New York   Toronto   London

To Michael Crichton, a man of many rare qualities and talents,
and the father of raptor-mania — D. L.

Acknowledgments

In addition to a thank-you for Dr. Currie's patient and
expert attention to this book, special thanks go to
Drs. Yoichi Azuma, Peter Dodson, James Kirkland,
Mark Norell, John Ostrom, and Altangerel Perle for
their kind advice. I am delighted that this subject
could lure talented artist David Peters back to
painting dinosaurs and attract the editorial skill of
Jackie Horne. I am grateful to both for their
enormous contributions to this book.

First Edition

Photography credits appear
on page 32.

Library of Congress Cataloging-in-Publication Data

Lessem, Don.
    Raptors! : the nastiest dinosaurs / by Don Lessem ,
illustrated by David Peters ; scientific adviser,
Philip Currie. — 1st ed.
        p.   cm.
Includes bibliographical references and index.
ISBN 0-316-52119-1
1. Velociraptor — Juvenile literature.   [1. Velociraptor.
2. Dinosaurs.] I. Peters, David, ill. II. Title.
QE862.S3L467   1996
567.9'7 — dc20   95-7110

10 9 8 7 6 5 4 3 2

SC

Published simultaneously in Canada
by Little, Brown & Company (Canada) Limited
and in Great Britain by Little, Brown and Company (UK) Lim

Reprinted by arrangement with Little, Brown & Compa
Printed in U.S.A.

AUTHOR'S NOTE

"You ought to write a book on raptors." That's what Steven Spielberg, director of the film *Jurassic Park,* said to me one day on the set of the movie. I was one of the film's science advisers, invited by Mr. Spielberg to help make sure that the dinosaurs in his movie looked as realistic as possible. Since he knows something about dinosaurs (and a great deal about what people like), I took his suggestion seriously.

I'd always been interested in raptors myself, though no more so than in any other types of dinosaurs. They *all* fascinate me. But a few days before my conversation with Mr. Spielberg, I had visited Stan Winston Studio, where the robot dinosaurs used in *Jurassic Park* were being made, and the moment I walked into the door, my interest in raptors became intense.

The dinosaurs were still in the early stages of construction. But even the rubbery, lifeless skin of a *Velociraptor* hanging on a coatrack was terrifying. Though it couldn't move, it *looked* ready to pounce, and for a moment I was truly frightened. I'd seen real raptor fossils before, as well as paintings and sculptures of the frightening beasts. And I'd even seen a few clunky raptor robots in museums. But when I saw that beautiful skin and stared into the *Velociraptor's* menacing eyes, I felt I was looking at a live dinosaur for the first time.

After seeing the *Velociraptor* brought fully to life in *Jurassic Park,* I became even more eager to learn as much as I could about the entire raptor family. I talked to my dinosaur-scientist friends and learned that several new and fantastic raptor dinosaurs had been discovered since *Jurassic Park* was made. The movie raptors and the new real-life ones inspired me to write a book about *all* the raptors. So here is the book Steven Spielberg asked for. I hope the facts about raptors, and the vivid illustrations of talented artist David Peters, will make these dinosaurs more real than ever in your mind's eye.

THE KILL Montana, 115 million years ago

In the soft twilight, a *Tenontosaurus* (teh-NON-tuh-SORE-us) is grazing on the edge of a lush forest. Nearly as long as a school bus, this dinosaur roams in search of food nearly all its waking hours. The *Tenontosaurus* is alert as it feeds, listening for the approach of any meat-eater, big or small. But it does not hear or see the keen-eyed hunters that are watching it hungrily from the woods.

Suddenly, silently, the killers attack. A dozen *Deinonychus* (dye-NON-ih-kus) leap out from the forest. Each killer is no bigger than a wolf. But by ambushing in a pack, a group of *Deinonychus* can take down the largest dinosaurs in their world.

Leaping and slashing with their razor-sharp claws, the *Deinonychus* rip open the tenontosaur's neck and belly.

In a bloody frenzy, the *Tenontosaurus* flails at the hunters with its huge tail and kicks out with its powerful limbs. It manages to crush several *Deinonychus*. But the pack continues its vicious attack. A few grim minutes later, the *Tenontosaurus* lies dead. The hungry hunters rip away slabs of meat with their sharp teeth until their appetites are satisfied. Other meat-eaters follow, to scavenge meat from the corpse. By dawn, all that is left of the *Tenontosaurus* is a few scattered bones.

The raptors have struck again.

WHAT IS A RAPTOR?

When many of us think of raptors, the vicious human-size villains of the book and movie *Jurassic Park* leap to mind. In the words of a *Jurassic Park* guard, raptors are "as smart as chimpanzees and as fast as cheetahs." But the book and film are fiction. Although it is based on science, *Jurassic Park* makes many dramatic exaggerations about dinosaurs.

The real raptor dinosaurs were no smarter than ostriches and no faster than poodles. Some raptors were also *smaller* than poodles. But other kinds of raptors, which have just

So what makes a dinosaur a true raptor, a member of the Dromaeosauridae? More than its name, its size, or the time when it lived. Raptors were two-legged animals with hollow bones like other meat-eating dinosaurs. And, like many other meat-eating dinosaurs, raptors had sharp teeth with notches like steak knives, which helped saw flesh.

But raptors evolved with several special characteristics all their own. They had especially narrow hip bones. Their tailbones were wrapped in tendons that made their tails stiff

recently been discovered, were as big as trucks.

The first raptor fossils ever found were discovered more than eighty years ago. But not many raptors have been found since. Raptor skeletons are rare. In any environment, meat-eaters are never as common as plant-eaters, because meat-eaters have a less abundant food supply than plant-eaters do. And the bones of raptor dinosaurs, like those of other small dinosaurs, were more likely to be scattered by wind and water than were the heavy bones of larger dinosaurs.

Scientists are still trying to determine what raptors are, where they came from, and what became of them. Spectacular new fossil finds, discovered only in the past few years, have forced scientists to change many of their ideas about how raptors looked and acted.

Not every raptor is a raptor dinosaur. Confused? The word *raptor* literally means thief. It's a name scientists usually use to describe birds of prey, such as hawks and eagles.

Paleontologists don't use the name *raptor* to describe the group to which these vicious little dinosaurs belong. They call them the Dromaeosauridae (DROH-mee-uh-SORE-ih-day). Dromaeosauridae are all small to medium-size meat-eaters that lived during the last of the three dinosaur periods, the Cretaceous, which lasted from 144 million to 65 million years ago.

as rods. Their hands were especially flexible for gripping. But raptors are most easily recognized by their killer claws, fearsome weapons on their inside fingers and toes. Long, curved, and narrow, these blades could be pulled up off the ground while the animal was moving. And, like switchblades, they could be snapped down and forward when the animal wanted to leap and slash at its victims.

Only raptors and their cousins, the little meat-eating Troodontidae (troh-uh-DON-tih-day), had oversize claws and strong, nimble hands.

But troodontids were not as strongly built in their feet and hands as raptors were, and they couldn't use their claws as powerful weapons. Among all dinosaurs, only raptors perfected the art of killing by hand and foot. Turn the page and meet them all — from the little *Velociraptor* and *Dromaeosaurus* to the bigger *Deinonychus,* the giant *Utahraptor,* and other still-unnamed huge raptors.

Raptors' teeth were not particularly large, but they were efficient. The back edge of each one was lined with serrations, like a steak knife, allowing the raptor to saw easily through flesh. ◄

The long tailbones of a raptor were encased in tough connective tissues called tendons. As a result, raptor tails were very stiff. Such a tail could have been used to help the raptor keep its balance while it stood on one foot and slashed with the other.
▼

Raptors had powerful shoulder muscles, which helped them hold on to their prey. ▲

The base of the pubic bone was tilted backward, more like the pubic bones of modern birds than those of other meat-eating dinosaurs. The large plate at the lower end of the pubic bone might have made an ideal sitting pad. ▲

The long fingers were each tipped with a deadly sharp claw well suited for snaring prey. ▲

◄ Hatchling raptors were very small. Only skulls have been found. They indicate that babies had short snouts and large eyes.

The killer claw on the second toe could be moved through a wide arc, similar to the movement of a cat's claw. While running, the raptor could raise the claw off the ground, which kept its tip sharp. The claw could be swung down during an attack to cut like a surgeon's scalpel. ◄

DROMAEOSAURUS: The First Raptor

The first raptor ever found may have been the last to roam the earth. Its name was *Dromaeosaurus* (DROH-mee-uh-SORE-us), which means "swift-running lizard."

Dromaeosaurus was just one of many dinosaurs discovered by Barnum Brown. Brown was a colorful character who wore a fur coat and carried a gold-topped cane. The son of a Kansas farmer, Brown began digging for dinosaurs while he was a college paleontology student. On a dig, he met scientists from the American Museum of Natural History, in New York, who offered him a job after college.

Brown worked for the American Museum until the day he died, sixty-six years later. During that time he hunted for fossils all around the world. He discovered more dinosaurs than anyone had before. His finds, including the first *Tyrannosaurus rex,* earned him the nickname "Mr. Dinosaur."

In 1909, a rancher from the Red Deer River valley, in Alberta, Canada, visited the American Museum. The rancher noticed how much the dinosaur bones on display in the museum looked like those he'd seen on his ranch, and he wrote a letter to the museum, which reached Barnum Brown. Brown was so curious to see the fossils that he visited the Red Deer River valley the next summer. He found a treasure trove of dinosaur bones there, and he returned each summer during the next few years to look for more fossils. The country was remote and hilly, so Brown used a river barge as his headquarters. He steered the barge downstream and stopped where he thought he might find fossils.

Barnum Brown

Sunday visitors to Barnum Brown's river barge

Since he had a great sense for fossils, he often found them, then dug them up and floated their enormous bones downriver to the railroad, where they were loaded for transport back to New York.

During the summer of 1914, Brown discovered part of the skull and several foot bones of a dinosaur that had not been known about before. Brown and a coworker named it *Dromaeosaurus.* From just its sharp teeth and large toe bones, scientists could see that this new dinosaur was a fierce and powerful little meat-eater. But it was a meat-eater unlike any other. In Brown's time, and until recently, all meat-eating dinosaurs had been divided into two groups: small and large. The small ones were called coelurosaurs (SO-loor-uh-sorz). The big ones were grouped as carnosaurs. The deep, rounded skull Brown found was shaped like the skull of a carnosaur. Yet it was much smaller than other carnosaur skulls. The size of its foot bones and skull indicated that *Dromaeosaurus* was not more than six feet long and was lightly built for speed. Some scientists called it a coelurosaur. But others thought it should be grouped with the carnosaurs.

While *Dromaeosaurus* was clearly different from other small dinosaurs that had been discovered before it, scientists had no idea it belonged to a group of killer-clawed dinosaurs we now call raptors. They were missing an important clue, since the foot bones found did not clearly show a raptor-type toe. Nor did many scientists think that *Dromaeosaurus* could be a vicious pack hunter, as we now think raptors may have been.

Since Brown's first *Dromaeosaurus* find, *Dromaeosaurus* teeth and bits of bone have often been found in the Red Deer River valley among the bones of larger dinosaurs. Some scientists suggested, as we now believe, that these smaller dinosaurs died while hunting, in a pack, fighting prey much bigger than themselves. But others dismissed this idea as implausible; they thought it more likely that the *Dromaeosaurus* teeth had simply been washed next to the big plant-eaters' skeletons after the *Dromaeosaurus* died.

Dromaeosaurus remained a mystery for decades. The badlands of western Canada have since proven to be the best dinosaur burial grounds in the world. Dozens of skeletons from thirty-seven different types of dinosaurs — more kinds of dinosaurs than are found in any other place on earth — have been unearthed in its hills and valleys. But no better fossils of *Dromaeosaurus* have been found in more than half a century.

The importance of *Dromaeosaurus* as the first of the raptor dinosaurs to be discovered was overlooked for more than fifty years. Not until two more raptors had been found — *Velociraptor* and *Deinonychus* — was *Dromaeosaurus* recognized as the first member of the raptors ever to be discovered.

NAME: *Dromaeosaurus albertensis* (DROH-mee-uh-SORE-us AL-ber-ten-sis)

MEANING: Swift-running lizard from Alberta

SIZE: 6 feet (1.8 meters) long (estimated)

SKULL LENGTH: 8 inches (203 millimeters)

WEIGHT: 50 pounds (23 kilograms) (estimated)

PERIOD: Late Cretaceous, 76 million to 72 million years ago

FOSSILS FOUND: Skull, parts of foot, isolated teeth, bone fragments

PLACE: Alberta, Canada

ENVIRONMENT: Warm, temperate floodplains, with a variety of habitats similar to those found in Florida today

POSSIBLE PREY: *Corythosaurus* (koh-RITH-uh-SORE-us) and other duck-billed dinosaurs; *Centrosaurus* (SEN-truh-SORE-us) and other horned dinosaurs, especially the small, old, and injured; mouse-size mammals; and small plant-eating dinosaurs

SKULL: The back of *Dromaeosaurus*'s skull is unusually wide. This broad skull may have helped give the animal additional biting strength. The ½-inch-long teeth of *Dromaeosaurus* are so thick that they are sometimes mistaken for those of a young tyrannosaur.

Dromaeosaurus had a narrow snout but broad cheeks, with room for both eyes to face forward. With both eyes focusing on the same image, *Dromaeosaurus* may have been able to see in three dimensions, an advantage in hunting and in grasping.

KILLER CLAW: A long, large claw that was believed to have come from this dinosaur may have actually come from another raptor dinosaur, *Velociraptor.* The dimensions of *Dromaeosaurus*'s claws, like those of much of its body, are unknown. It might have had a short sickle-shaped claw. One researcher has suggested that short claws may explain why it needed an especially strong skull and big teeth — to kill its prey.

BUILD: The foot bones of *Dromaeosaurus* suggest it was heavily built for a raptor dinosaur, perhaps a better leaper than runner.

VELOCIRAPTOR: The Smallest Raptor

Which was the meanest raptor of them all? Perhaps the smallest, *Velociraptor* (veh-LOS-ih-RAP-tor), which means "swift hunter."

Roy Chapman Andrews with the first nest of dinosaur eggs ever discovered

A skull, parts of two bodies, and a "killer" hand claw of *Velociraptor* were discovered in 1922. They were found in Asia's remote Gobi Desert on a great expedition led by the real-life Indiana Jones. His name was Roy Chapman Andrews. Like Barnum "Mr. Dinosaur" Brown, Andrews worked for the American Museum of Natural History. He came to the American Museum as a janitor and finished his career as its president. He led expeditions in search of whales, bears, and other exotic animals in Korea, Japan, and India. Like Indiana Jones, he wore a jaunty hat, carried a revolver, and had a terrible fear of snakes.

In the early 1920s, Andrews and his crew ventured to the remote Gobi Desert of Mongolia in search of ancestors of modern humans. Instead, they found dinosaurs. Andrews's scientists discovered not only *Velociraptor* but many bizarre dinosaurs. They also discovered the first nest of eggs ever known to be those of dinosaurs. Andrews's dinosaur discoveries cre-ated a public frenzy. Thousands volunteered to go on his expeditions, and upon his return, ticker-tape parades were held for him across the country. To benefit the museum, Andrews auctioned off a single dinosaur egg for five thousand dollars.

Andrews was eager to do more exploring in the Gobi. But the Mongolians were angered that Andrews had sold their fossil treasures. After 1925, Andrews was not permitted to return to Mongolia. Unfriendly Communist governments in the region continued to keep out Western scientists for decades.

The famous "Fighting Dinosaurs," locked in mortal combat

PROTOCERATOPS

But in 1971, a team of Polish scientists explored the Gobi Desert. Two paleontologists, Halszka Osmólska and Teresa Maryańska, discovered what may be the most spectacular fossil discovery ever made: "The Fighting Dinosaurs." In the soft sands of the ancient desert, a *Protoceratops* (PROH-toh-SARE-uh-tops) and a *Velociraptor* were found, locked in battle for life. As they wrestled, a sandstorm may have suffocated them both. The Polish scientists uncovered the dinosaurs' skeletons, still locked in combat 80 million years later.

Dr. Halszka Osmólska (right) with fellow paleontologist Dr. Kielan-Jaworowska

VELOCIRAPTOR

Dr. Teresa Maryańska at an excavation in Mongolia

13

The complete skeleton of the *Velociraptor* told scientists much more about the appearance of this raptor and about the relationship of meat-eating dinosaurs to their living descendants, birds. Unlike most dinosaurs, which had riblike scales to support their stomachs, *Velociraptor* had large bony plates, similar to those of modern birds.

The *Velociraptor* found with the *Protoceratops* was battling its prey with grasping claws, about to make its kill. But a more recent *Velociraptor* find gives even greater evidence of this raptor's vicious habits.

In the early 1990s American Museum scientists returned to the Gobi. Among their discoveries, Dr. Mark Norell and his colleagues found a *Velociraptor* skull with a small hole in its top. Dr. Norell noticed that the tooth of another *Velociraptor* would have fit exactly into that hole. *Velociraptor*s fought not only other dinosaurs but other *Velociraptor*s, too! Were these two *Velociraptor*s fighting over a mate, or competing for food? Or did one intend to eat the other? Scientists aren't sure. But they do think that one *Velociraptor* killed another with a bite through the skull.

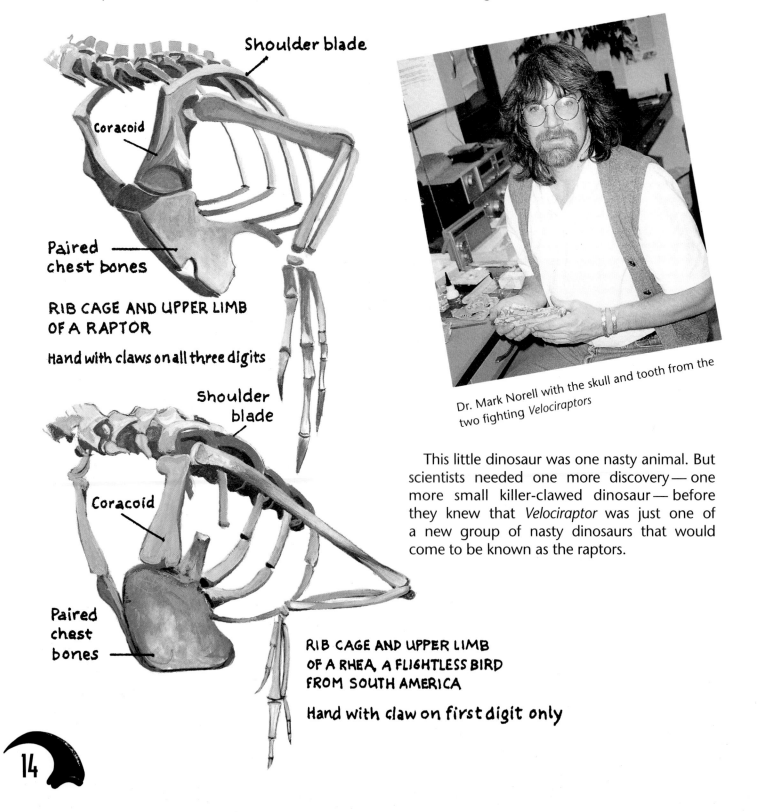

Shoulder blade

Coracoid

Paired chest bones

RIB CAGE AND UPPER LIMB OF A RAPTOR

Hand with claws on all three digits

Shoulder blade

Coracoid

Paired chest bones

RIB CAGE AND UPPER LIMB OF A RHEA, A FLIGHTLESS BIRD FROM SOUTH AMERICA

Hand with claw on first digit only

Dr. Mark Norell with the skull and tooth from the two fighting *Velociraptors*

This little dinosaur was one nasty animal. But scientists needed one more discovery — one more small killer-clawed dinosaur — before they knew that *Velociraptor* was just one of a new group of nasty dinosaurs that would come to be known as the raptors.

INSIDE ▶ VELOCIRAPTOR

NAME: *Velociraptor mongoliensis* (veh-LOS-ih-RAP-tor mon-go-lee-EN-sis)

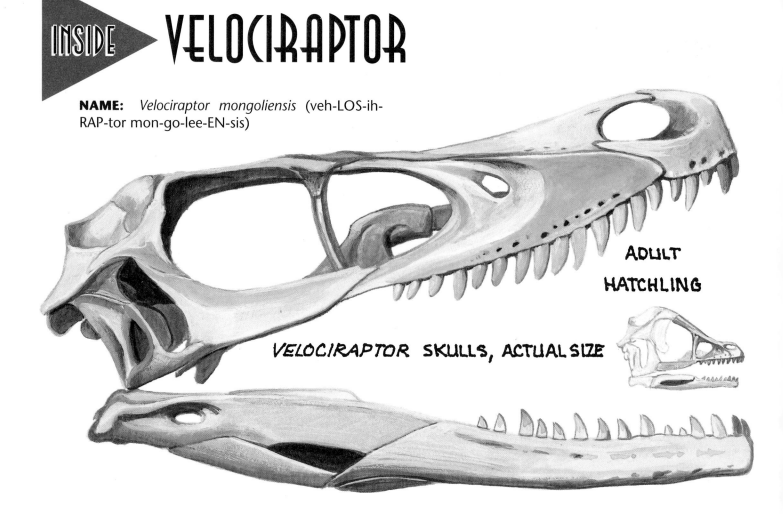

ADULT

HATCHLING

VELOCIRAPTOR SKULLS, ACTUAL SIZE

MEANING: Swift runner from Mongolia

SIZE: 6 feet (1.8 meters) long

SKULL LENGTH: 7½ inches (191 millimeters)

WEIGHT: 25 pounds (11 kilograms)

PERIOD: Late Cretaceous, 85 million to 80 million years ago

FOSSILS FOUND: Several partial and complete skeletons

PLACE: Mongolia; China; perhaps Russia and western North America

ENVIRONMENT: Dry valleys with streams and some desert conditions, including sand dunes

POSSIBLE PREY: *Protoceratops,* a sheep-size member of the horned dinosaur family (though it had no horns), and *Oviraptor,* a toothless meat-eater. Small mammals and other dinosaurs were also possible victims. Without especially powerful claws or jaws, this raptor may have relied more on its speed, its gripping hands and its intelligence to capture prey not much larger than itself.

KILLER CLAW: The curved and grooved second toe claw was 3¼ inches long (8 centimeters). But in life it was covered with a horny sheath, like all dinosaur claws. This sheath may have increased the length of its claw to 4 inches or more. Compared to its size, these are average claws for a raptor, though large for any other dinosaur.

SKULL: *Velociraptor* had a lower, narrower head than those of other raptors. Its ⅜-inch-long teeth were sharply grooved and unevenly set in its long jaws. Its eyes and brain area were large for a raptor. These features suggest it was a smart and keen-eyed dinosaur. The size of its brain compared to its body size suggests it may have been about as smart as some birds and certainly smart enough to hunt in packs.

RUSSIA

MONGOLIA

VELOCIRAPTOR DISCOVERY SITE

CHINA

TAIWAN

BUILD: *Velociraptor* was especially long-limbed and lightly built for a raptor. It was likely the fastest of the raptor dinosaurs, though not nearly as fast (nor as big and smart) as *Jurassic Park* makes it out to be. According to footprint evidence, the fastest known dinosaurs, the ostrich-like ornithomimids, ran 25 miles per hour. That's about as fast as the fastest human. *Velociraptor* probably did not run quite that fast. It may not have run at all! Mongolian scientist Altangerel Perle has suggested that *Velociraptor* hopped like a kangaroo on its powerful hind legs. While we have no proof of how *Velociraptor* moved, other scientists think Dr. Perle may well be right. However it moved, it was built to be one of the fastest, smartest, and deadliest animals in its world.

DEINONYCHUS: The Killer-Claw Hunter

The discovery of the human-size *Deinonychus* was the key to scientists' current understanding of raptors as a group and to a changing view of all dinosaurs.

Dr. John Ostrom

In 1964, Dr. John Ostrom, a paleontologist from Yale University, was prospecting for dinosaurs in the badlands of central Montana. Walking across a steep, bare hillside, Dr. Ostrom came across a large, curved claw on a three-fingered hand. He knew immediately that he'd discovered a new kind of meat-eating dinosaur. Next he found a complete and perfectly preserved foot with a huge toe claw. But it took him and his crew several years to dig deep into the hillside and find more fossils of these animals. As they dug, Dr. Ostrom's team uncovered parts of other of these meat-eaters, as well as the dinosaur they were attacking, a twenty-three-foot-long plant-eater called *Tenontosaurus.*

Ostrom named this small dinosaur *Deinonychus* in honor of its amazingly large and deadly claws. He speculated that several members of a pack of *Deinonychus* had been killed in an attack on a *Tenontosaurus* and that sand from a stream had covered over parts of their bodies. More digging in recent summers at the site has uncovered still more

Deinonychus, suggesting that ten or more *Deinonychus* may have been in on the kill, with many dying in the vicious struggle.

Before the discovery of *Deinonychus,* scientists had not been certain that raptors were a separate group of dinosaurs. The only other raptors, *Dromaeosaurus* and *Velociraptor,* were not very well known among dinosaur paleontologists. Fossils of the two dinosaurs had not been carefully compared to each other or to other meat-eaters, large or small. *Velociraptor,* with its killer claw, resembled *Dromaeosaurus's* fossils in many ways, but the claws of *Dromaeosaurus* weren't known.

After the discovery of *Deinonychus,* however, it was clear there was a group of small killer-clawed meat-eaters that lived in both Asia and North America. In 1969, dinosaur paleontologists Edwin H. Colbert and Dale Russell placed *Deinonychus* and *Velociraptor* in a group with *Dromaeosaurus* in the larger category to which *Dromaeosaurus* had long been the only member, *Dromaeosauridae.* These are what we now call the raptor dinosaurs.

The discovery of *Deinonychus* changed more than just the way scientists grouped a few dinosaurs. It led paleontologists to a whole new way of thinking about all dinosaurs. Since dinosaurs had first been discovered, the public and many scientists thought these prehistoric creatures were sluggish, cold-blooded animals. But Dr. Ostrom realized that *Deinonychus* must have been an active, graceful animal to wield its killer claws in battle. This dinosaur needed plenty of energy for repeated, rapid movement. Cold-blooded animals, which rely on their environment to control their body temperature, cannot keep up such activity. So, Dr. Ostrom concluded, at least some dinosaurs, especially *Deinonychus,* may have been warm-blooded, like their close cousins, birds.

For nearly twenty years, scientists considered *Deinonychus* the biggest and earliest of all the raptor dinosaurs. But in just the last few years, new discoveries have changed that view completely.

NAME: *Deinonychus antirrhopus* (dye-NON-ih-kus an-tee-ROH-pus)

MEANING: Terrible claw, counterbalancing (referring to its stiff tail)

SIZE: 10 feet (3 meters) long

SKULL LENGTH: 1 foot (305 millimeters)

WEIGHT: 100 to 150 pounds (45 to 68 kilograms)

PERIOD: Late Early Cretaceous and early Late Cretaceous, 119 million to 93 million years ago

FOSSILS KNOWN: Several complete and partial skulls and skeletons

PLACE: Montana; Wyoming

ENVIRONMENT: Flat river deltas with lush plant life and warm weather, much like the Mississippi River delta today

POSSIBLE PREY: *Tenontosaurus*, other plant-eating dinosaurs, and all mammals

KILLER CLAW: 5 inches (13 centimeters) long, and in life, perhaps 1 or 2 inches longer, when covered with a horn sheath. The toe joints are especially flexible, so the killer toe could be pulled up and back while the dinosaur ran and flexed far forward and down to slash at prey.

SKULL: *Deinonychus* had a large, lightly built head with big openings on the sides where jaw muscles attached, facilitating both snapping and crushing. Its teeth were large and curved backward, well built for tearing meat by tugging as the strong jaws bit down. A hinge behind the eyes may have worked as a shock absorber so that *Deinonychus* didn't jar its brains when it bit down hard. *Deinonychus* had large eye sockets, suggesting that it had big eyes. Like many dinosaurs, *Deinonychus* had a bony ring in the iris of its eyeball for support.

BUILD: *Deinonychus* was as long as a tiger and as heavy as a large wolf but stood no taller than an eight-year-old child. Half of its body length belonged to its stiff tail, hardened by bony rods that reached to its tip — an unusual feature of raptors. This tail probably helped balance the animal while it leapt and slashed with its toe claws.

Deinonychus's head sat on a slim and flexible neck. Its arms and shoulders were powerfully built, enabling its long clawed arms to hold on to struggling prey. The hands of *Deinonychus* were unusually long and strong, good for slashing and gripping. Pebble-size, crescent-shaped bones in the wrist were arranged in such a way that *Deinonychus* could fold its big hands easily.

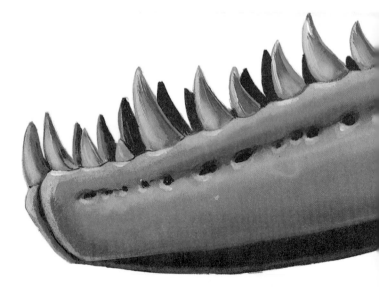

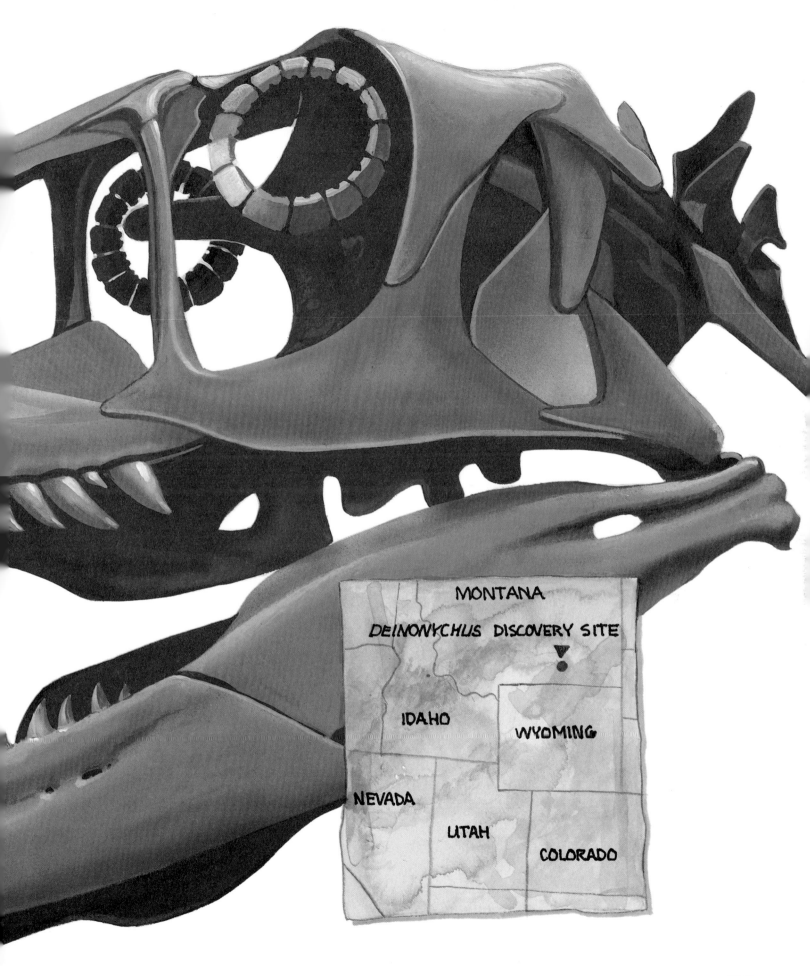

THE GIANT RAPTORS

Dr. Philip Currie is the world's expert on meat-eating dinosaurs. He's probably the only person alive who can identify any meat-eater from a single tooth. He digs for dinosaurs and works in a museum in the world's richest dinosaur graveyard—the same area of Alberta, Canada, where Barnum Brown discovered the first raptor dinosaur. Dr. Currie also travels the world, digging for dinosaurs and examining what other scientists have found.

In 1989, Dr. Currie's travels brought him to Mongolia. There, in the office of one of Mongolia's dinosaur scientists, Dr. Altangerel Perle, Dr. Currie saw a skeleton that astonished him. Discovered by Mongolian scientists during an expedition in the Gobi Desert, the bones formed a nearly complete skeleton of a raptor. Yet it wasn't the completeness of the skeleton that surprised Dr. Currie but the animal's size. At almost twenty feet long, this skeleton was more than *twice* the size of any known raptor dinosaur!

In 1991, Dr. Currie traveled to Japan, a country with a great love for dinosaurs but few fossils of its own. Dr. Yoichi Azuma, a Japanese paleontologist, showed Dr. Currie a site west of Tokyo where he had discovered scattered dinosaur

A claw from the giant raptor found in Japan by Dr. Yoichi Azuma

bones. Dr. Azuma had found these bones during one of the most elaborate excavations ever undertaken for dinosaurs. In an area just a few blocks wide, Dr. Azuma and his crew had bulldozed and dug out a cliff face nearly seventy feet high. Inside they found teeth and bones of several dinosaurs, including one bone Dr. Currie recognized as a part of the jaw of a raptor. From its size, Dr. Currie could tell that this, *too,* belonged not to a human-size raptor but to a giant nearly twenty feet long. Later digs at the site have uncovered a claw and other fossils from the same kind of giant raptors.

When the American Museum resumed its dinosaur hunts in the Gobi Desert in the 1990s, Mark Norell and his colleagues also found skeletons of giant dromaeosaurs, similar to the one in Dr. Perle's office.

Dr. Philip Currie in Mongolia

As I write this book in 1995, neither the Japanese nor the Mongolian giant raptors have been officially named, though they are certainly new kinds of animals. And there are at least two new raptor dinosaur discoveries in Montana and South Dakota. Often it is years from when a dinosaur is first dug up to when it is named. First the bones must be thoroughly cleaned and studied. Then a researcher writes a paper for a scientific journal describing what is unique about the dinosaur and giving it a scientific name. Usually the name is a Latin or Greek word for a special feature of the dinosaur or where it was found, or simply the name of a scientist. When the paper is published, the name becomes official and is reported to the press. So be on the lookout for news of the names of these new raptor dinosaurs—they may already have names by the time you read this!

The dig site west of Tokyo where Dr. Azuma and his crew discovered a giant raptor jawbone

UTAHRAPTOR: New Giant Raptor

One newly discovered giant raptor already has a name. It comes not from Asia but from North America.

In the summer of 1991, Dr. Jim Kirkland and his family were having lunch in the desert town of Moab, Utah. Dr. Kirkland is a dinosaur paleontologist and an expert on the dinosaurs of Colorado and Utah.

Dr. Kirkland eats fast. So while his wife and daughter were finishing their pancakes, he decided to visit the rock shop next door. A store clerk showed him some armor plates from an ankylosaur dinosaur that had been dug up in eastern Utah. The fossils of this plant-eater resembled those of armored dinosaurs Dr. Kirkland had been digging up at the time, and he decided to put together a team to explore the site where the armor plates had been found.

That summer, Dr. Kirkland's team found parts of many ankylosaurs at the site. They also found bits of teeth and jaws from meat-eating dinosaurs. The remains of scavengers and predators are often found among the bone beds of plant-eating dinosaurs.

Dr. Jim Kirkland holding a Utahraptor hand claw

Just as Dr. Kirkland was about to close the quarry for the winter, crew member Carl Limoni yelled to him, "I think I found a rib!" Dr. Kirkland asked Carl to dig farther. Soon Carl realized this was not a rib at all but an enormous sickle-shaped claw!

During several summers of digging at that site and at another in Utah, Dr. Kirkland and his teammates discovered many more parts of giant raptors—pieces of skull, snout, legs, feet, hands, and tail.

By 1993, Dr. Kirkland had enough evidence to declare a new raptor dinosaur, which he named *Utahraptor*. *Utahraptor* was truly a frightening animal. Longer than a station wagon and as heavy as a polar bear, it flashed some of the largest sets of meat cleavers ever seen in nature on its hands and feet.

Paleontologists were surprised by the news of *Utahraptor* and of the giant raptors discovered in Asia. Scientists hadn't guessed that such huge versions of these nasty dinosaurs had ever existed.

Were the giant raptors the nastiest dinosaurs ever? Dr. Kirkland thinks *Utahraptor* might have been. But other dinosaur scientists disagree. Dr. Currie thinks *Utahraptor* was too heavily built, and so too slow-moving, to be very terrifying. Even among raptors, Dr. Currie thinks *Utahraptor* was less frightening than the much smaller but swifter *Velociraptor*.

UTAHRAPTOR

NAME: *Utahraptor ostrommaysi* (YEW-taw-RAP-tor OS-trom-MAY-zee)

MEANING: Utah hunter, plus a combination of two names: that of scientist John Ostrom and of Chris Mays, founder of Dinamation, Inc., a robot dinosaur company

SIZE: 20 feet (6 meters) long

SKULL LENGTH: Unknown

WEIGHT: 1,000 pounds (450 kilograms)

PERIOD: Late Early Cretaceous, 125 million years ago

FOSSILS FOUND: Parts of skull, snout, teeth, legs, feet, hands, and tail

PLACE: Utah

ENVIRONMENT: Dry savanna-like environment with some palmlike trees and streams and lakes

POSSIBLE PREY: Four-legged plant-eaters up to 60 feet (18.3 meters) long, iguanodontids, other dinosaurs large and small

KILLER CLAW: Hand claws 10 inches (25 centimeters) long. Toe claws 11 inches (28 centimeters) long.

SKULL: Judging from the fragment of the front of the jaw that has been found, *Utahraptor* had a powerful jaw and large, serrated teeth. Without more skull remains, though, it is difficult to tell how strong its senses were or how large its brain might have been.

BUILD: *Utahraptor* was very powerfully built, with leg bones as thick as the much larger *Allosaurus* (al-uh-SORE-us). Dr. Kirkland thinks it was too big and heavy to leap and kick like smaller raptors and may have stood on one leg and kicked with the other, while slashing with its arms, like a karate fighter.

UTAHRAPTOR

VELOCIRAPTOR

KILLER CLAWS COMPARED, ACTUAL SIZE

DEINONYCHUS

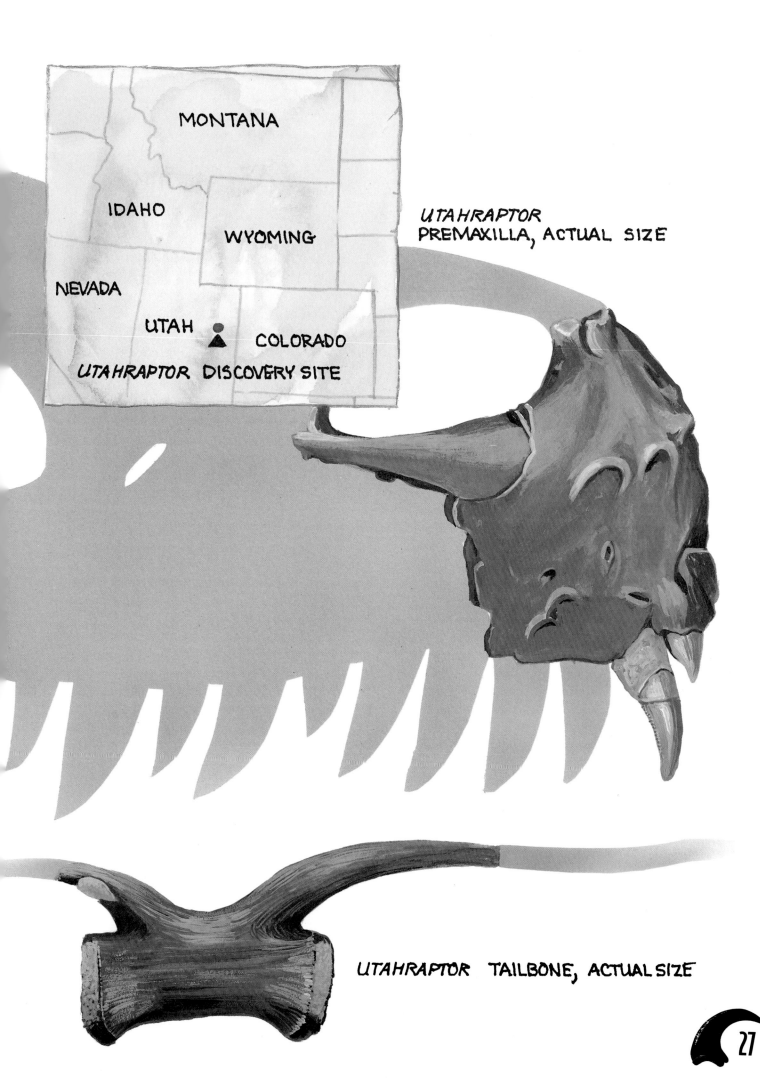

MONTANA

IDAHO

WYOMING

NEVADA

UTAH COLORADO

UTAHRAPTOR DISCOVERY SITE

UTAHRAPTOR
PREMAXILLA, ACTUAL SIZE

UTAHRAPTOR TAILBONE, ACTUAL SIZE

27

MORE RAPTORS?

Dinosaur science changes quickly. On average, a new kind of dinosaur is discovered every seven weeks. No doubt there will be other raptors discovered soon. And dinosaurs that have already been discovered but not yet studied may yet prove to be raptors.

One such animal recently found to be a raptor is *Saurornitholestes* (SORE-or-NITH-uh-LES-teez), "lizard bird-robber" a six-foot-long (1.8 meters) meat-eater from Canada. It's the smallest adult dinosaur ever discovered in western Canada.

A farmer who lived near an Alberta fossil preserve found its teeth and skull and other bones in 1974. Nearly complete skeletons of *Saurornitholestes* discovered in western Canada in 1989 and in Montana in 1990 show it was a raptor dinosaur, virtually identical to *Velociraptor.* Dr. Currie and some other researchers think *Saurornitholestes* actually *is Velociraptor.*

From Asia come fragments of other raptor dinosaurs. *Adasaurus* (ad-uh-SORE-us), named for a legendary Mongolian evil spirit, a six-foot-long (1.8 meters) meat-eater with a small killer claw, lived after *Velociraptor.* Bits of a single skull and body are the only fossils of this dinosaur that have been found. *Hulsanpes* (HOOL-san-peez), "foot from Hulsan," a dinosaur that also lived in Mongolia, after *Adasaurus,* is known only from a piece of a foot! But its foot is nearly identical in structure to the feet of other raptor dinosaurs.

Sometimes dinosaurs that scientists thought were raptors prove to be something else entirely. In North America, the little (seven-foot-long) meat-eater *Chirostenotes* (kye-ROS-tuh-NOH-teez), or "narrow hand," had been considered a raptor for many years, because its long arms resembled those of *Deinonychus.*

But its foot, which was discovered in 1979, belonged to a much more heavily built animal than any raptor and lacked a killer claw. Now it has been placed in a different group of meat-eaters, the elmisaurs.

Other dinosaurs have *raptor* in their names but do not belong to the raptor family. *Eoraptor* (EE-oh-RAP-tor), which means "dawn thief," is the name given in 1993 to one of the earliest of all dinosaurs. A primitive meat-eater the size of a dog, it lived in Argentina 228 million years ago, long before the killer-clawed raptor dinosaurs evolved.

Oviraptor (OH-vih-RAP-tor) lived in the same time and place as a true raptor dinosaur, *Velociraptor.* Both were discovered by the American Museum crew of Roy Chapman Andrews in rocks nearly 80 million years old, in the Gobi Desert of Mongolia. *Oviraptor* is an odd toothless member of the meat-eating dinosaurs, not a true raptor dinosaur.

Oviraptor's name means "egg thief," a name chosen by Andrews's team because its bones were found on top of a nest of dinosaur eggs, one of the first nests ever found. Andrews's scientists assumed the eggs must belong to *Protoceratops,* the small plant-eater that was the most common dinosaur found in the Gobi. And they also assumed the toothless meat-eater was stealing the eggs.

But *Oviraptor* had been misnamed, as American Museum scientists found out nearly seventy years after Andrews's discovery. In 1994, the museum's dinosaur scientist, Dr. Mark Norell, announced that he had found a nest of eggs of the type thought to belong to *Protoceratops.* The top of one of the eggs had eroded, exposing the tiny bones of an unborn dinosaur. Dinosaur embryos are very rare. The beautiful bones found by

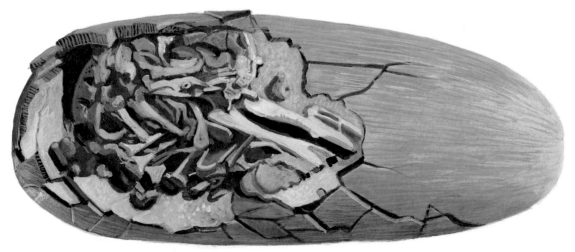

OVIRAPTOR EGG, ACTUAL SIZE

Dr. Norell belonged to one of the most complete embryos of a meat-eating dinosaur ever found. And they proved to be the bones not of a *Protoceratops* but of an *Oviraptor*.

What does this mean? *Oviraptor* was not stealing *Protoceratops's* eggs as the Andrews team thought. Instead, *Oviraptor* was a caring parent, tending to its own eggs.

Perhaps the true raptor dinosaurs were good parents, too. Until we find their nests, eggs, and embryos, we won't know for sure.

Dr. Norell made another surprising discovery near where he found the *Oviraptor* eggs: two tiny skulls of young *Velociraptors*. Were these tiny raptors hunting for eggs? Or were they the prey of the *Oviraptor*? Or was the *Oviraptor* also raising the *Velociraptors* along with its own young, just as many birds will care for young of another species placed in their nest? For now, scientists cannot be sure how those raptors died or why they were found so near the *Oviraptor* nest. But Dr. Norell thinks that the way both young *Velociraptors* were found, with their skulls crushed and their bodies missing, suggests that they were killed by the *Oviraptor* to feed to its young. For once, it seems, raptors were the victims instead of the killers.

RAPTORS: Coming and Going

What dinosaurs were the ancestors of raptors? And do raptors have any living descendants? Did they simply disappear, like so many other types of dinosaurs? Or did they evolve into a new type of animal?

It is difficult for scientists to figure out which dinosaurs evolved from which, or when or why those changes happened. No group of dinosaurs lasted throughout the 165 million years of dinosaur time, and no single kind of dinosaur is known to have existed for more than a few million years. Since we know only three hundred kinds of dinosaurs from all of the dinosaur days, we cannot be sure of the

But by the middle of the Cretaceous period, the newest, most sophisticated line of big killer dinosaurs was emerging: the tyrannosaurids. Even the largest raptors were no match for these strong-jawed, keen-eyed, smart, and graceful giants. So the big raptors disappeared. But the smaller raptors, such as *Velociraptor,* lived on as smaller, swifter killers with lighter appetites than *T. rex.* By 75 million years ago, little raptors such as *Dromaeosaurus* and *Saurornitholestes* were rare, among the last survivors of the raptor line.

Although raptor dinosaurs are extinct, their close cousins live on today. We call them birds.

history of any one dinosaur group, especially a group as mysterious as the raptors.

Scientists are just beginning to figure out a little about the origin of raptors—a very important and puzzling group of dinosaurs. Most groups of predators seem to produce larger and larger species over time. The last of the several kinds of tyrannosaurs, for example, was the biggest meat-eater of them all, *Tyrannosaurus rex.* But the earliest raptors we know are the giants. The last raptors are among the smallest of their kind.

How could this be? Some scientists think that raptors, like many other kinds of meat-eaters, came from small ancestors. *Ornitholestes* (OR-nih-thuh-LES-teez), "bird robber," was a North American meat-eater from the late Jurassic period, a world dominated by huge meat-eaters such as *Allosaurus.*

At the end of the Jurassic period, *Allosaurus* appears to have died out, at least in North America and Asia, which were connected during much of dinosaur time. *Ornitholestes* or another small meat-eater may have evolved to become the giant raptors such as *Utahraptor,* filling in the gap left by the extinct *Allosaurus.*

Most scientists now consider small meat-eating dinosaurs from the Jurassic period to have been the ancestors not only of many dinosaurs such as the raptors, but of all birds. *Archaeopteryx* (ar-kee-OP-ter-ix), the earliest known bird, lived at the end of the Jurassic period. Its skeleton is nearly identical, except for the feathers, to a small meat-eating dinosaur, *Compsognathus* (komp-sug-NAY-thus). The hollow bones, light skulls, and long three-toed legs found in meat-eating dinosaurs are all features of modern birds, too. The next time you eat a chicken leg, think of the chicken's close relative, a raptor dinosaur. But instead of you biting *its* leg, it would probably be trying to take a bite out of *you!*

Raptors are long gone. But they were far from failures. Instead, they were among the most varied and successful of killer dinosaurs. They created and perfected one of the nastiest weapons nature has ever given an animal— the killer claw. We can all share in the continuing excitement of discovering raptors. And we can all breathe easier knowing that raptors live now only in the movies.

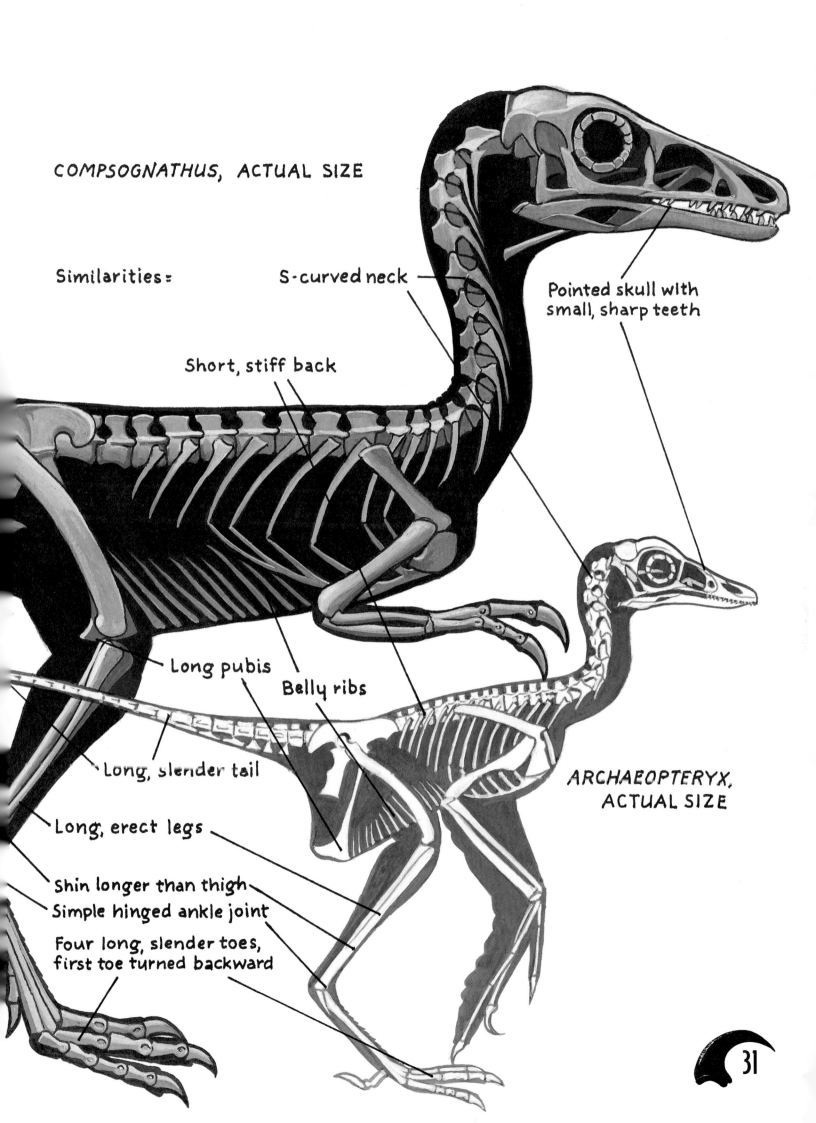

COMPSOGNATHUS, ACTUAL SIZE

Similarities:

S-curved neck

Pointed skull with small, sharp teeth

Short, stiff back

Long pubis

Belly ribs

Long, slender tail

Long, erect legs

Shin longer than thigh

Simple hinged ankle joint

Four long, slender toes, first toe turned backward

ARCHAEOPTERYX, ACTUAL SIZE

FOR FURTHER READING

Michael Benton. *Deinonychus.* New York: Kingfisher, 1994.

David Lambert. *The Dinosaur Data Book.* New York: Avon, 1990.

Don Lessem and Donald Glut. *The Dinosaur Society Dinosaur Encyclopedia.* New York: Random House, 1993.

William Lindsay, illustrated by Guiliano Fornari. *The Great Dinosaur Atlas.* New York: Simon and Schuster, 1991.

Dr. David Norman, illustrated by John Sibbick. *The Illustrated Encyclopedia of Dinosaurs.* New York: Crown, 1985.

Helen Roney Sattler. *The New Illustrated Dinosaur Dictionary.* New York: Lothrop, Lee, Shephard, 1990.

Monty Reid, illustrated by Jan Sovak. *The Last Great Dinosaurs.* Edmonton, Alberta: Discovery Books, 1992.

OTHER RESOURCES

Dinosaurus magazine. 505 Eighth Avenue, 18th Floor, New York, NY 10018. A monthly magazine for kids about dinosaurs.

Dinosaur Productions. 84 Moffat Road, Waban, MA 02168. A commercial source for inexpensive replicas of *Utahraptor* and *Velociraptor* claws as well as casts of many other dinosaur fossils.

DIGGING RAPTORS

Dinamation International, a nonprofit arm of the Dinamation Corporation, runs dinosaur digs in the area where *Utahraptor* was discovered. Children as young as five can participate with their parents. For information, write Dinamation at P.O. Box 307, Fruita, CO 81521.

ABOUT THE AUTHOR

"Dino" Don Lessem digs dinosaurs. He is the founder of the international nonprofit Dinosaur Society and its children's newspaper *Dino Times,* as well as the dinosaur columnist for *Highlights for Children* magazine. Mr. Lessem has written and hosted *NOVA* documentaries and was an adviser to the film *Jurassic Park.* He is a consultant to television series and museums and an exhibit and CD-ROM creator. His dinosaur books for adults include *Dinosaurs Rediscovered, The Complete T. rex* (with Dr. John R. Horner), and *The Dinosaur Society Dinosaur Encyclopedia* (with Donald F. Glut). His most recent children's books are *Inside the Amazing Amazon; Troodon: The Smartest Dinosaur; Ornithomimids: The Fastest Dinosaurs;* and the National Science Teachers' Association recommended books *The Iceman; Jack Horner: Living with Dinosaurs;* and *Digging Tyrannosaurus rex* (with Dr. John R. Horner). When not at home in Boston with his family, Mr. Lessem participates in dinosaur expeditions to Mongolia, Argentina, Montana, and Arctic Alaska.

ABOUT THE ILLUSTRATOR

Artist David Peters made a splash in the world of children's books with the publication of his first title, *Giants of Land, Sea & Air—Past & Present.* Mr. Peters has since written and illustrated several other books for children, including *Strange Creatures* and *From the Beginning: The Story of Human Evolution.* For the past few years, he has shifted his focus from painting to sculpture, but the chance to illustrate a book about raptors lured him back to children's books. Mr. Peters makes his home in St. Louis.

PHOTOGRAPHY CREDITS

Pages 8 and 12: Negatives/Transparencies #19508, #18541, and #410734, Courtesy Department of Library Services, American Museum of Natural History. Page 13: Courtesy of Halszka Osmólska and Teresa Maryańska. Page 14: Photograph by Don Lessem. Page 18: Courtesy of T. Charles Erickson, Yale University, Office of Public Affairs. Page 22, top: Courtesy of Dr. Yoichi Azuma. Page 22, bottom: Courtesy of Alan Bibby. Page 23: Courtesy of Philip Currie, Royal Tyrrell Museum of Palaeontology. Page 24: Photograph #BR 982 by François Gohier, courtesy of François Gohier Pictures.

TRIASSIC PERIOD
245 MILLION YEARS AGO

JURASSIC PERIOD
▼208 MILLION YEARS AGO

240   230   220   210   200   190   180   170   160

UTAHRAPTOR

VELOCIRAPTOR

VELOCIRAPTOR ▼

AHRAPTOR ▼   DEINONYCHUS ▼ DROMAEOSAURUS ▼

ETACEOUS PERIOD
MILLION YEARS AGO

TERTIARY
PERIOD
65 MILLION
YEARS AGO

40   130   120   110   100   90   80   70   60   50

DEINONYCHUS

DROMAEOSAURUS